The Greeks

History of an Ancient Advanced Culture

Life in Ancient Greece

by Niels Lobmann

Table of Contents

I. An Early Advanced Culture

Ancient Greece is the birthplace of much of Western knowledge and many sciences. This applies to philosophy, where we find Socrates, Plato and Aristotle, as well as to literature, such as the immortal dramas of Sophocles. It also applies to mathematics where we find Pythagoras and Euclid, and it applies to the historiography of Herodotus. Last but not least, we owe our Olympic Games to the "ancient Greeks" and, to a large extent, even our political regime, democracy. The concept of a universe that consists of atoms was first thought of by Democritus, and many of our scientific approaches come from Thales of Miletus and his successors. Archimedes already had early technical and physical knowledge. Our Latin alphabet also comes from ancient Greece, where it was introduced by the Phoenicians in the 8th century B.C.

The geographical location of the Greek peninsula had a great influence on the culture of its inhabitants. On the mainland, equipped with manageable natural resources and surrounded by the sea, over time they increasingly integrated the sea into their living conditions. About 80 percent of the Greek mainland is made up of mountains, and only smaller waters run through the landscapes. This offers few possibilities for productive agriculture. This is why the Greeks had the idea early on to turn the neighboring islands into colonies. They settled along the Anatolian coast (areas of today's Turkey). They became professional in all aspects of seafaring, and they developed into experienced traders. Since they had plenty of raw materials for stone constructions and also had qualified knowledge and skills, some of the most impressive constructions of antiquity originated from them, e.g. the **Arkadiko Bridge** and the stone relief "**Therapeutae of Asclepius**". The ancient Greeks reached a peak in almost all areas where human learning is possible.

The earliest evidence of the Greek culture can be found in the **Stone Age**. In the **caves of Petralona and Franchthi**, two of the oldest sites in human history, there is evidence of settlement. Between 6000 and approx. 2900

B.C. Greece was already the homeland of many people who settled and pursued agricultural activities. They began to keep domestic animals and became farmers. They built stone houses consisting of a room covered with wood held together by clay.

II. The Cycladic Culture

The Cycladic culture, which began around 3200 B.C., was an early golden blossoming age in ancient Greece. On the **Aegean islands**, including Delos, Naxos and Paros, settlements were created, which testify to the fact that the inhabitants lived there continuously and which belong to the oldest evidence of human sedentariness. Not only houses, but also temples made of hewn stone were built. People survived on fishing and trade. Art and architecture developed at an ever-increasing rate. And the last phase of this civilization can hardly be distinguished from the first Minoan one.

III. The Minoan Culture

The Minoan culture (from about 2700 to 1500 B.C.) developed on the **island of Crete**. The name came from the archaeologist Sir Arthur Evans, who discovered the **Palace of Knossos** of the Cretan king **Minos** in 1900 B.C. What the inhabitants called themselves is unknown. Crete quickly became the leading maritime power in the region. In general, this civilization was growing and flourishing, just like the Cycladic civilization. There is no data to determine whether it even existed before it, but this is considered possible by experts.

The Minoans developed a writing system, which is known as **Linear A**. The hieroglyphs have only been partially deciphered to this day. They made great progress in shipbuilding, construction and the manufacture of ceramics, as well as in art and science. They also developed strategies for warfare. **King Minos** was described by the ancient historians (e.g. Thucydides) as the first to put together a competent fleet of ships to occupy the Cyclades (a group of islands in the Aegean). It is unclear whether he conquered or colonized them.

The Minoans built several palaces in which the ruling class were concentrated. There was also a complex social structure that could not be reconstructed exactly. King Minos had the most extensive palace complex. After the original was destroyed by an earthquake, the complex was rebuilt even more extensively and elaborately. The ruins can still be visited today. On more than 20,000 square meters there were at least 1200 rooms, distributed over approximately five floors. The rooms, stairs and corridors were richly and partly preciously decorated. Since the rooms were arranged around an inner courtyard, the construction of the palace must have looked like a maze system to people unfamiliar with the place. In addition, the building had modern heating and drainage systems. There were bathrooms with seat tubs, flushing toilets and a heating system with warm water. All the rainwater was collected in cisterns.

Crete was generally prosperous; taxes were levied that ran up in the palace. The granaries of the palace were full to bursting, and there were plentiful supplies of food such as oil and honey.

A **myth** was created around King Minos, which is still narrated to this day. According to this myth, he received a beautiful bull from the god Poseidon, which he was to sacrifice to Zeus, the father of the gods. He could not bear to do it and exchanged the magnificent animal for another. This in turn earned him an outburst of wrath from the supreme God. He made Minos' wife fall in love with the bull and let him mate with her with the help of a wooden cow. The result was a monster called Minotaur, who loved human flesh. Because of this life-threatening characteristic, the king held him in a labyrinth. Every year seven unmarried young men and women were locked up in the labyrinth, where the bull killed the human sacrifice. In order to spare their own island people, all the young people were taken from Athens. An Athenian took this opportunity to offer himself as a victim. Equipped with a ball of wool and a dagger, which the king's daughter Ariadne gave him, he first defeated the beast and then found his way out of the labyrinth using the thread. Then he escaped with the ruler's daughter. Because of this story we still speak about the **Ariadne thread** to this day.

In the last phase of Minoan civilization, most of the palaces faced destruction. What caused the destruction is unclear. It could have been an earthquake or a hostile attack from the Greek mainland. Many parts of Minoran cultural life were later hardly to be distinguished from the Mycenaean culture.

IV. The Mycenaean Culture

The Mycenaean culture (from approx. 1900 to approx. 1100 B.C.) was regarded as the beginning of Greek culture. It established itself on the mainland. Apart from Crete, the first European advanced culture could be found here. The inhabitants were the **Archaeans**. Their architectural progress was remarkable. The writing system was further developed into **Linear B**, an early form of the Greek alphabet. Religious rites established themselves, many of which were adopted by the Minoans of Crete. There were Earth and heaven goddesses and gods who already formed the basis for the later world of gods. The Mycenaean culture was named after the **Mycenae** Center. As is typical for other centers, this was divided into an upper and lower town, whereby the upper town was constructed like a fortress. The characteristic features of this cultural epoch are the elaborate buildings constructed for graves and entire grave complexes. The dead received vessels as grave goods. The inhabitants created numerous ceramic works of all kinds.

There was a multi-layered social structure. The center was always a **palace** in which a **king** resided who acted as head of administration. The **supreme commander** of the army was subordinate to him. This team of two held the political and economic power in their hands. There was a huge bureaucracy, which had to work on clearly separated areas. Fiscal taxes had to be controlled and administered, the army had to be structured and the economic conditions organized. This included an overview of the commercial transactions but also of the well-filled warehouses located in the palace.

The fall of the Mycenaean culture took place between 1200 and 1100 B.C. The large cities in the southwest were abandoned. Some historians assume that the **Dorian invasion** was an essential cause. Accordingly, the Doric Greeks advanced as far as Peleponnes and the archaeans had to retreat. This was possible because the Dorians were already advancing with riding squadrons and fighting with superior weapons. Other historians assume that this was not or not only the cause of the downfall. Problems that affected the structure of the society could have contributed to this, as could other events that destroyed the system. There is no archaeological evidence or preserved documents that could provide a clear explanation. In any case, all the major metropolises collapsed, almost throughout Greece, and at a rapid pace.

The fall was inevitable because the palaces collapsed or were destroyed. The highly developed writing system was almost completely lost. The social system collapsed and the economic power declined sharply. The road networks perished because they were no longer used or maintained. The population decreased.

The authority then passed to the army leaders as kings, who exercised a tyranny (dictatorship). From these rulers came **basileus**, a term used for Greek monarchs. A time of warlike and destructive activities began and introduced the Dark Ages.

V. The Dark Ages (approx. 1200–800 B.C.)

In the Dark Ages, people's living conditions became more difficult. People did not starve to death, but access to food sources was very important. Livestock breeding was used to eat the meat. The next stage, which is the processing of wool, was hardly reached by anyone. Those who had the largest herds could rule. Many inhabitants emigrated and settled elsewhere, for example in Asia Minor.

Nevertheless, there were small areas in which the old life was maintained to a considerable extent and the culture continued to be cultivated. Jewelry made of gold and glass was produced and used as merchandise. In other parts of Greece, settlements developed at the same time, e.g. **Athens**, **Corinth**, **Olympia** and **Troy**. They were able to establish themselves as **centers**, and in the course of the 8th century B.C. the Dark Ages were overcome.

VI. The Archaic Period (approx. 800–500 B.C.)

At the beginning of the Archaic period the most important strata were **the aristocracy**, **the peasants** and **the slaves**. The basic elements of society were the "**oikos**". It was a kind of manor or farm that was the home of a group of people. It consisted of the aristocrat, his wife and children, his agricultural helpers and servants, and free people who were loyal to him. In times of peace their task was to help in house, yard and field and in times of war and plunder to support their patron. In addition to that, slaves belonged to the society.

Goods and chattels were the essential **status symbols**. Every aristocrat strove to increase his material possessions. Warlike acts and raids of other ethnic groups were not taboo because they increased their own prosperity. In order for their own status to be duly appreciated, the aristocrats were regularly invited to a banquet. They gave each other expensive gifts and also held **tournaments**. There was social cohesion among one another.

At the same time there were a lot of farmers who lived on a farm but which was much smaller. They were free people but had to work hard to secure their living conditions. It was not enough to cultivate and harvest useful plants; they had to be processed into final products on the farm. From time to time taxes were paid to the aristocrats.

In some areas there was still the basileus. The basileus stood principally above the aristocrat and was the supreme decision maker in legal matters, and he was also authorized to appoint the National Assembly, in which only aristocrats were allowed to speak and had rights.

VII. Polis Cities

After the Dark Ages, agriculture was back on track. It became worthwhile again to own land and cultivate crops. This led to the expansion of the urban centers, which became stronger. Now the time had come for polis to become the **basis of the political system** in the greater history of Greece. This continued through not only the Archaic period but also the Classical period. The main characteristic of the polis was the **self-government** of its citizens. They were independent and not politically dependent on any other groups or governments. Several of them developed from the existing centers. A particularly impressive polis emerged in **Athens**.

Although a polis was a city state, it consisted of both the urban area and the surrounding countryside, which included agricultural land and a network of roads. The central place for the political activities of the inhabitants was the **agora** (market and meeting place), where people met regularly. Here, current events and topics were discussed, which strongly promoted the social cohesion of the community. Temple complexes and town hall buildings were found in the local proximity, so the people were only a short distance away from important facilities. Each polis was divided into a kind of district, called a **phyle**, in which the inhabitants were officially registered. There were **councils**, **magistrates** and corresponding office holders who had precisely defined areas of responsibility. Through the use of the **National Assembly**, citizens could exercise influence on political events. The polis basically strived for **autonomy** and equality of people before the law. Each polis, however, differed from the others in the way in which they carried out offices, as they were independent entities. The exercise of offices and participation in political assemblies was reserved for male adult citizens everywhere.

VIII. Athens

Historically, the best knowledge about the organization of the city states was found in Athens. Here in the polis, the powerful basileus first became the highest **office holder**. There was an administrative apparatus headed by the **archon**, while the **polemarchos** was the supreme commander of the army. In the course of the development there were several **archons**. These were government officials elected by the National Assembly. The National Assembly was the main legislative authority because it made the laws. The **Areopagus** was the supreme jurisdiction. It also conducted foreign policy in the name of the city state. It also controlled the administrative officials. The members of the Areopagus and the archons were basically **aristocrats**. They also had the right to speak in the National Assembly.

IX. Sparta City

In Sparta there was the **Gerusa**, the council of the elders. It consisted of elderly gerontes who remained in charge for the rest of their lives. They did not need to legitimize themselves to anyone with their decisions. They also represented the supreme judges. They were elected by the National Assembly. There were traditions that say that in the election the loudness of the shouts was decisive, not the number of votes.

X. Draco

By the **end of the 7th century B.C.** there was a decisive change in legislation. The Athenian **Draco** gathered the regulations and laws that circulated and structured them. The result was a much clearer set of rules that was comprehensible and strengthened the state as a punitive force. He took action against vendettas and advocated that the level of punishment for criminal acts should be determined by the courts. He banned extreme, inappropriate punishments, which were often imposed, from the regulations. He also separated intentional homicide from unintentional homicide. He supported the development of differently specialized courts with jurisdiction over different types of offences. In order for everyone to know the laws, he had them published in the marketplace. Today we still talk about **"Draconian Measures"**, meaning inappropriate penalties. This does not do justice to the reformer who, on the contrary, introduced a **fairer jurisdiction**, which fought arbitrariness and ensured a better balance between offences and penalties.

XI. Solon's Legal Reforms

The gap between the rich and the poor in Athens became wider and wider as only the aristocracy really ruled and passed laws in their favor. Many farmers, fishermen and shepherds found themselves in precarious conditions. Debtors became servants and in the worst cases enslaved. Those who already owned little land were severely affected by periods of drought. Therefore many Greeks emigrated and settled in parts of Sicily, the south of Italy, on islands or on the Black Sea coast. Also the North African **Cyrene** (today in Libya) and today's **Marseille** originated in this way. The **colonization** took place partly peacefully, partly warfully, depending on the conflict or agreement with the population that was already living there. Other politically independent urban centers developed in which different political conditions prevailed, from polis to terrorist regimes. An example of this was the tyrant **Cypselus** of Corinth, who seized power in the middle of the 7th century and murdered or expelled many citizens of Corinth.

In order to prevent social unrest and stabilize the situation, **Archon Solon** imposed drastic decisions in 594 B.C. First of all a general debt relief came into force. Debtors could no longer be made servants if they could not pay, and farmers who were enslaved because of their debts became free men again. Parts of the Athens Constitution were changed. Citizens were given more rights in the National Assembly; rules and regulations were posted in the temples.

The society was also redefined by defining **classes**. The first class consisted of large landowners and merchants, the second of craftsmen, larger farmers, producers and merchants, the third of smaller farmers, craftsmen, merchants and fishermen, and the fourth of wage earners. Rights were decreasing from class to class, so the rich still had the most control. Despite this, the new constitution was a step forward because the **majority voting system** was introduced.

Solon also made economic and social policy decisions. To stabilize the economy, he banned the export of grain but supported the export of wine and oil products. Citizens who did not do any work lost their rights. By law, the elderly had to receive care from their children.

XII. Cleisthenes' Legal Reforms

In spite of the reforms, powerful men in individual polis continued to seize power, even in the important metropolis of **Athens**. The last tyrant in the city state was **Hippias**, who was overthrown with the help of the Spartans. But his tyranny was hardly over when the aristocracy began to fight for power. The nobles were anxious to improve social conditions and to promote social cohesion because people were becoming increasingly dissatisfied, especially because the number of inhabitants had increased enormously so peace in the country ought to have been secured. But who could ensure this?

Cleisthenes prevailed and issued a new constitution **around 510 B.C**. It guaranteed that all free citizens of Athens were equal and could become office holders at any level. Then there was a **people rule**. It was carried by the male inhabitants of Athens, whereby only the father of the family was allowed to become politically active. The female and enslaved

Athenians remained without rights, as did the resident trading foreigners. Those who held office received financial compensation (regime). This ensured that the lower classes could also participate.

The **balance in power** here was as follows:

- The **Council of 500** was responsible for all matters of state. It was composed of elected citizens. The electoral constituencies were divided taking into account the interests of urban, rural and coastal residents. The four strata were equally divided and delegated. The Council should make all arrangements for meetings of the National Assembly. The head of state changed every day with the help of a lottery.

- The **Ecclesia (National Assembly)** was the legislative authority. It was also the controlling body for the ruling council and the military. The civil service, the judiciary and the army officers were appointed by election. It was responsible for deciding whether to wage war. It ensured that no dictatorship or even new tyranny arose by deliberating every year on the expulsion of people who had made themselves politically suspect. Before someone could rise to autocracy, he must leave the country for a full decade. However, this would be agreed beforehand. Here a piece of pottery entered into a game, which presented the name of the possible perpetrator. This is why we speak today about **ostracism**.

- The **People's Court** would conduct the trials. Whoever wanted to join the People's Court had to be elected by the National Assembly.

In addition to structuring the social order, craftsmanship was developing rapidly. Greek pottery was very popular and sculpture grew and prospered. On the **Aegean** island, a **payment system** in the form of coins was established.

XIII. The Greco-Persian Wars

The reforms of Cleisthenes had the effect of increasing the cohesion of society. This meant that the strength of the state and the military was growing again. The Greeks succeeded well in defending themselves against attacks from abroad and also in expanding their own territory. They could cope with the conflicts with the Persians.

In the 6th century B.C. the Persians brought some cities in Asia Minor under their control, in which Ionians were settled. There were conflicts between Persians and Ionians, which culminated in the **"Ionian Revolt"** in **494 B.C**. The Athenians rushed to the aid of the Ionians when the Persians turned against them. They succeeded in regaining control of the Ionian sites and destroying the city of Miletus. Then they planned revenge on the Greeks and later even envisaged the subjugation of the whole of Greece.

First they attacked the Greeks in the year **492 B.C**. on both land and water. But the weather conditions led to heavy seas in which the Persian fleet sank. Two years later, they attacked again. They had with them the extyrant Hippias, who had found shelter with them. He was to be installed as ruler in Athens. First they overran the city state of Eretria, and then they settled their camp near Marathon. Militarily they were superior to the Athenians, so they called the Spartans for help. They didn't come fast enough. The commander **Miltiades** faced the battle with the Persians before they reached Athens. There was a **battle at Marathon**, in which the Greeks won and the Persians pushed back to Asia Minor.

During the rule of Miltiades the Greeks expanded their fleet considerably. This led to many men entering military service so that the warships could be occupied. This strengthened the young democracy because not only did members of the nobility perform military service but citizens did too.

While the first attacks had been commanded by the Persian **Grand King Darius I**, his successor **Xerxes I** planned the next campaign against the Athenians, who, however, did not miss the plan. They founded the **Hellenic Alliance** to defend against them. In 480 B.C., the Persians attacked again. They came through the Hellespont (today's Dardanelles) to the mainland. Xerxes achieved partial success by winning the **Battle of Thermopylae** (a narrow point between the sea and central Greece, which today is largely silted up) and he overran central Greece. Attica was cleared at the last second by the Greeks before the Persians invaded. The Athenian commander **Themistocles** then allied himself with the Spartans who, together with the attacked Greeks, defeated the Persian invaders by water. This happened in the **Battle of Salamis**. These two battles are regarded as decisive historical events that had a far-reaching influence on the course of European history. If the Persians had won, **Europe** could have undergone a completely different cultural, religious and political development.

Xerxes was back again in his Asian territory. But he still didn't give up his plan to conquer Greece. In Thessaly, which lay in northern Greece, he prepared a campaign on the mainland. In 479 B.C., the Persians arrived in Attica and almost razed it to the ground. But the Spartans intervened. Under the leadership of Pausanias, they finally defeated the Persians in the **Battle of Plataea**. During these events, the Ionians of Asia Minor were liberated from Persian rule and several islands of Asia Minor were incorporated into the Hellenic Alliance.

XIV. The Age of Classicism

1. The Basis of the Rise of Greece

The Age of Greek Classicism extended **from 480 B.C. to the time of Alexander the Great (356–323 B.C.)**. The end was sometimes considered to be the birth but often also the death of Alexander. After that the Hellenistic period established itself.

The important foundations for the economic rise of Greece were laid by the victory over the Persians. The Greeks became aware of their strength and power. The time period considered a golden age began for the country. Athens was growing into a great power.

A decade earlier, Persia's attempt to subjugate Athens had failed. As a visible sign of victory, the great politician **Pericles** had the **Acropolis** building, which had been destroyed by the Persians, rebuilt by the sculptor **Phidias**. In 490 B.C., he made a grandiose speech that went down in history. In it he praised the brave soldiers who achieved victory. In this it was said, for example, "So these men have shown themselves worthy of our city and fought bravely; the rest are to pray for a safer life, but they are not to be less courageous towards our enemies. Rather, you must see how powerful our city really is and love it with the devotion of your heart."

At the same time, the system of polis favored economic success. Since living conditions were economically secure, the Greeks could now devote themselves intensively to art and culture. Greece produced poets and thinkers as well as artists and cultural workers of immortal fame. The democratic order stabilized. The humanities and natural sciences were developing, which gave rise to doubt about the creation of the world by gods. People searched for the meaning and origin of life in the world and in the whole universe.

Nevertheless, in Greece it was not only joy and sunshine that reigned. On the one hand the good model of the city states with a lot of freedom and development possibilities had led on the other hand to individual polis fighting each other, especially Athens and Sparta. Since the common enemy Persia was eliminated, the two were in strong competition with each other. So even the golden age could not exist without fierce conflicts and struggles.

2. The Philosophy

In the favorable conditions of economic stability, many Greeks devoted themselves to philosophical considerations. They wrote down their intellectual achievements and passed them on to their pupils. Entire branches of knowledge emerged, above all philosophy. In antiquity, this term was used to describe many things that came to light in completely new ideas.

The term **philosophy** was derived from the Greek words "philo", which means love, and "sophia", which means wisdom, and therefore literally means nothing other than love for wisdom. Science, however, explored much more profound topics, namely the meaning and explanation of human existence in this world. Western philosophy began in the ancient Greek city of Miletus (now Turkey) with **Thales of Miletus**. He was the first to consider the original material of the universe from which we are all formed. Other great Greek thinkers were dedicated to philosophy, which found its highest expression and genius in Sophocles, his disciple Plato and his disciple Aristotle. The mathematician and mystic **Pythagoras** was the first to call himself a philosopher.

The branches of the ancient Greek philosophy are:

- **Metaphysics**: The science of existence. It deals with the principal laws that make existence possible and the discussion of whether and what meaning it has. It also includes the questions of whether there is a creator of the world and a soul and whether there are constant structures or conditions of being that are not subject to any change. For example, this includes the question of whether the human being basically has free will.

- **Epistemology**: The theory of knowledge. It asks how we can actually know, what we know, what exactly "knowledge" is and why we have it. It also includes legitimate doubting of assertions. Plato said, for example, that people do not learn at all but only remember already existing knowledge that slumbers in the imperishable soul until it receives an impulse to become accessible.

- **Ethics**: The science of human (morally correct) action. An important study in this field was written by Aristotle, who wanted to show his son the right way to conduct himself in life. Ethics is about morally acceptable behavior, the way in which a person should live, and the basis on which his decisions are made.

- **Politics**: The science of governance. This does not only mean mere governance but includes the important questions of how to behave as a good citizen, how to be a good neighbor and what to do to the community in which you live. The first study on this science was published by Aristotle.

- **Aesthetics**: The science of art. It is about the perception and feeling of beauty and the fundamental question: What is it that makes something "beautiful"? Plato and Aristotle were committed to finding objective criteria, while other philosophers took the view that something is beautiful when someone finds it beautiful and that all these evaluations are purely subjective.

3. The Daily Life

Of course, most people lived a completely normal life, which was considered commonplace at that time. The cities were protected by stone walls. Most of the land within these massive borders was private property with private households. Like all early civilizations, Greece was dominated by **agriculture**. Most farmers lived in manageably large farms and were able to make a living from their yields. They cultivated olives, various types of grain, wine, vegetables and fruit. Farm animal husbandry was common, with sheep, goats and cattle herds, and there was abundant fishing. The highest prosperity consisted in owning one's own land. Everyone tried to make a livelihood in as many areas as possible, such as baking bread and tailoring. At the same time there were a lot of temples and places of work for craftsmen. Among them were goldsmiths and manufacturers of stone and ceramic objects. Typical were workshops with one owner, one or two assistants and one slave. At first, the craft was little respected, but it improved its image over time because the products became more and more popular in the markets. Merchandise was one of the factors that increased prosperity and became the solid foundation of the economic system. The number of migrant workers also increased, favored by a stable currency. The resources of raw materials were systematically extracted and the infrastructure improved, above all by expanding the road system.

There were **free and unfree people**. The male citizens with their family members and Greeks from other cities as well as foreigners were free. Slaves were not free unless they were released. In every city there was an upper and middle class consisting of rich farmers, doctors and teachers. The largest part of the population, however, consisted of small farmers, craftsmen and slaves. Slavery was common; the number of slaves was estimated at 30% of the population. The number was so high because prisoners were often turned into slaves. Every child born of a slave was automatically a slave. But there were also slave markets abroad where they could be bought like cheap goods. They were regarded as linguistically gifted animals. Only the poorest inhabitants could not afford them. Every owner had the right to hit them with a whip. If they were lucky enough to live in a rich household, they were usually well treated. Those who worked in mines had the worst lives. There were also professionals among them who worked as doctors or civil servants for the common good. Those who did good work were often released. But also most free people had to work hard and did not have a high standard of living.

With the boom of the economy, the demand for **skilled workers** grew and they flowed more and more into the cities. Here they enjoyed great prestige and a good legal status by virtue of their skills but were not allowed to buy land.

A **child** was not considered a person until he or she was five days old. Parents were allowed by law to abandon their children and let them die during this time. Sometimes an outsider would take in the expelled child. In this case the child automatically became his slave. When the family accepted their child, they held a special ceremony and integrated him/her into the family.

4. The Women

The Greeks worshipped both gods and goddesses, and women took part in religious festivals. But in domestic life they were separated from the men. They usually lived in the rear or upper part of the house. In a rich family, the woman was expected to manage the household and often the finances. She did not go shopping; she stayed at home and sent the slaves to the market. The poorer women could not afford that. They had to go to the traders themselves and help their husbands with farming in addition to the household. Every woman had to spin, weave and tailor. In principle the woman was subordinate to the man and had fewer rights, but she was nevertheless a free person and could lead a free life. Some women were owners of inns, sold food or perfume, or weaved wool for a living. A girl usually married at the age of 15, with the wedding often arranged by her parents.

The Sparta women stood out in the women's rights category. They had the same rights to do business as men and were equal in many ways. They were free to choose their spouse. They owned a good part of the land in Sparta. It was well known, however, that other Greek women sometimes also owned land, for example in Thessaly.

There were many great women in ancient Greece. Examples are the famous poetess **Sappho** in the 6th century B.C., the philosopher **Arete of Cyrene** (approx. 400 B.C.) and the astronomer **Aglaonice** (approx. 150 B.C.).

5. The Olympic Games

The Olympic Games were held in the Sacred Grove of Olympia every four years for about five days. However, historical sources assume that they took place in every Greek city. They were part of a religious celebration. The first are believed to have taken place in 776 B.C., the last in 393 A.D. Athletes competed exclusively **in honor of Zeus** and not to perform at their best. They were not honored with medals but with a crown of leaves. The male participants came from all parts of the rural areas and from the colonies. In order not to burden the participants unnecessarily with clothing, they competed undressed. Spectators were also men and some single women. Disciplines were boxing, wrestling, running, horse racing, chariot racing and the pentathlon spear, discus, jumping, running and wrestling. If the games coincided with a time of war, the fighting was suspended so that everyone could participate. Women were not allowed to take part in the Olympic Games but they had their own competition, dedicated to the goddess **Hera**, which also took place every four years.

6. The Residential Buildings

The Greeks lived in simple, modest houses. They built them out of clay blocks, which they covered with plaster. The roofs were made of clay tiles. There were windows but no glass, so the walls simply had holes. The inhabitants shared one, two or three rooms. Only the rich lived in houses with more rooms. They were typically laid around an inner courtyard. Often there was an upper floor where the bedrooms and a room for the women were located. In this "**gynaecium**" the inhabitants made clothes and also ate. For the men there was the dining room called the "**andron**", which was on the ground floor where the living room was located. Even in the houses of the rich, the furniture was economical and purpose-built. The Greeks kept their various household items in wooden chests or hung them on the walls. Wealthy homeowners had a chest of drawers on which they presented their expensive crockery. People liked to lie down on their couch, which also served as a bed if needed. It consisted of a simple wooden frame in which ropes were stretched. Mats or blankets were laid on it. They began the day at sunrise and went to bed at dusk. The rich had lamps with olive oil for lighting.

7. The Nutrition

For ordinary people, bread was the main meal. They baked it from barley. Those who could afford it ate wheat bread. There was also sheep's cheese. Other common components of the food were fish, chicken, eggs and vegetables. Every household had pulses, onions, garlic and olives. The farmers also caught small birds to eat. They also ate raisins, apricots, apples, pears and pomegranates. The usual drink was water. Those who could pay for it sweetened it with honey. Wine was also popular and widespread. It was mixed with water. The wealthy class had a richly laid table. Here were found delicacies like roasted rabbits, peacock eggs and iris blossoms pickled in wine vinegar.

8. The Clothing

Despite the warm climate, the Greeks attached importance to clothing that covered the entire body. Women wore a "peplos". This was a rectangular piece of fabric that was folded and stapled together and extended to the feet. It was tied at the waist. Later there was the "chiton", a long but not so heavy **tunic**. Over it they wore the "himation", a cloth that served as a coat. Jewelry was popular with women; there were necklaces, bracelets and foot clips in many forms. They did not cut off their hair unless they were in mourning. Rich women used a parasol to protect their skin.

Men wore simple wool tunics that were tied at the waist. They also had a himation to wear over them. On their travels they put on a hat with a wide brim. In addition to wool, linen was also used for clothing. Rich people could also afford tunics made of cotton and silk.

Most of them were washed by means of a washing vessel called a "louterion", which was placed in a sheltered area. Wealthy households had a bathroom. They were rubbed with olive oil, which they then rubbed off again with a special tool, the "strigil". Afterwards, they were washed with water.

9. The Education

The **boys** learned reading, writing and mathematics but were also taught literature and music. The Greeks believed that physical education was particularly important and therefore taught dancing and athletic sports. The male children were taught at home from an early age and went to school from the age of six. This was often in the teacher's house. On the way to school they were accompanied by a slave who was responsible for their safety. Discipline was the top priority and the children were often beaten.

The **girls** were taught by their mothers at home. They learned mainly weaving and spinning. Some girls were also taught reading and writing. Women from higher classes were often very well educated, while poorer families could not pay for the lessons.

The education in **Sparta** was known to be particularly hard. At the age of seven, the boys had to move out from home to live in barracks. There, they were brought up to be soldiers from an early age. They were deliberately given little to eat so that they could learn to thieve in order to acquire cunning, tricks and malice. If they were caught, the punishments were harsh. For each offence they were beaten. The Spartan girls learned dancing and athletic sports because they were to become strong and healthy mothers for many soldiers. Our current term "Spartan" comes from these times.

When the Greek children had free time, they enjoyed ball games. The balls were made from inflated pig bladders. They also had bones as playing material, especially knuckles. There were spinning tops that could be turned. Girls played with dolls and boys with figures representing horses and wagons.

10. Literature, Art and Music

The Greeks are known for their great dramas. Probably the origin for this lay in groups that sang and danced in the honor of the god Dionysus (god of wine). Around 534 B.C., **Thespis** came up with the idea of adding a soloist to the choir who acted. Then a second and third soloist followed. So choral singing became the first drama. The actors acted on the raised stage, while the choir members stood in the foreground and commented on the scene. All actors were men. They wore masks on which the characters and their qualities were made visible. The audience sat in several rows in a semicircle. Our modern word "theater" comes from this time with the "**theatron**", which means "place where people listen". Greek tragedy is characterized by the fact that the main character is desperate or dies. The reason was that there was an error or an irreconcilable contradiction, but not because someone was acting mean or evil. An example is the drama *Antigone* by **Sophocles**. Antigone wanted to bury her brother, who died in battle, according to divine law. But the ruler Kreon followed the worldly laws according to which he was a traitor and therefore could not be buried. So there was an elementary conflict between divine and worldly laws. This antique play was often interpreted and is still performed to this day. Other great playwrights include **Aeschylus**, **Aristophanes** and **Euripides**.

The Greeks created grandiose lifelike sculptures. Among the greatest sculptors were **Praxiteles** and **Lysippos** (both in the 4th century B.C.) and above all **Phidias** (490–430 B.C.). One of the Seven Wonders of the World, the **statue of Zeus** in Olympia, with its stately size of 12 metres, originated from there. Other well-known examples of the great architecture were the marble figure **Venus of Milo**, which was created around 100 B.C. by an unknown master, and the **Laocoon group**, the original of which was not preserved in antiquity and was copied by the sculptors Hagesandros, Polydoros and Athanadoros from Rhodes (1st century B.C.).

Greek musical art liked to show scenes from mythology and everyday life. In the 6th century B.C., black-glazed figures were painted on a red background. From about 520 B.C. the colors were changed. Now there were red figures on a black background. This style became known as **red figure vase painting**. The Greeks also painted their urns with figures on a white background. The painting of walls also enjoyed great popularity with the artists, but unfortunately little of this has been saved.

11. The Architecture

Symmetry played an important role for the Greeks. The artists spared no effort to work out the right dimensions and proportions. There were three different styles, **Doric, Ionic and Corinthian**. The most important temples had porticoes in one of these styles.

The **Doric** columns were relatively short and wide. Their height was six times the diameter of the base. In principle, they were quite simple, but they already had flute-like grooves, i.e. vertical furrows, as a decorative element.

The **Ionic and Corinthian** columns had a height corresponding to nine times the diameter of their base. Both had a pronounced so-called capital, which is the upper end of the column. Ionic columns had spiral ornaments, while Corinthian specimens had leaves.

The most famous example of Greek architecture is the **Parthenon** in Athens. The construction of the temple began in 447 and lasted until 438 B.C., with the last decoration work only being completed a few years later. This was a short period of time compared to how long construction usually took in ancient times.

12. The Religion

The Greeks believed in the existence of several gods. They imagined that the male and female deities were, generally speaking, and behaved like humans. Therefore their behavior was not always exemplary and sometimes even really bad. Among the most important were:

- **Aphrodite**: Goddess of Beauty and Love

- **Athena**: Goddess of Wisdom, Art and Science

- **Artemis**: Goddess of Hunting

- **Ares**: God of War

- **Dionysus**: God of Wine, Music, Dancing and Theater

- **Demeter**: Goddess of Fertility

- **Hephaestus**: God of Blacksmiths and Fire

- **Hermes**: Messenger of the Gods

- **Hestia**: Goddess of the Hearth

- **Poseidon**: God of the Seas

- **Apollo**: God of Poetry and Prophecy

These gods lived in Olympus. They were headed by **Zeus**, the most powerful figure of the gods, who had his wife **Hera** at his side. She was the goddess of marriage, birth and family. The couple of gods was also resident in Olympus. One of the gods worth mentioning was **Hades**. He was the inhuman god and ruler of the realm of the dead, where the souls of the dead lived. Hades was also the name of the underworld as well.

Each city had several temples where people gathered to pray. In the courtyards there were altars where crops were offered and animals were sacrificed. Many private people also possessed an altar in the courtyard of their estate, where they made sacrifices to the gods.

When a person died, his body was either buried or burned, with the ashes subsequently buried. The grave was given food, drink and parts of household goods, as well as personal belongings, so that the deceased would not lack anything. However, only wealthy families could afford this. The family members visited the grave from time to time and offered sacrifices there.

The Greeks believed that after death the ferryman **Charon** rowed the souls over the **Styx**. This was the river bordering the underworld. Since this crossing had to be paid for, they placed coins on the dead person's eyes or under his tongue. Poor families sometimes couldn't afford that. But if the journey across the river remained unpaid, the soul had to stay on the riverbank until the end of time. If the soul succeeded in the underworld, then it would be judged there and sent to **Elysium**, Heaven, or **Tartarus**, Hell, depending on the judgment. Those who had been evil all their lives must of course go to Hell, while especially good people would go to Heaven. However, this would be very likely only for true heroes. Many people were to be assigned to mediocrity. They came to an intermediate level, which was not extreme but rather boring and cloudy. Offering sacrifices at the grave made the place friendlier for the deceased.

Living people were not allowed to enter Hades, and the dead were not allowed to escape. This was ensured by the hellhound **Zerberus**, who was always ready to fight and had three heads to defend himself against intruders or refugees.

Since the torments in the hell of Hades were said to be unimaginably great and no one wanted to land there, the majority of the Greeks were very anxious to live their lives honorably and sincerely.

13. The Weapons of the Military

The Greek army was based largely on infantry whose soldiers were called **hoplites**. They had to pay for their equipment and weapons themselves, which is why most of them came from the middle class. They wore helmets, a shield to protect their chest and back, and greaves. They were armed with an approximately two-meter-long wooden spear with a metallic tip. They also carried swords and daggers. When they went into battle, they formed a **phalanx**, a line in which the shields overlapped to form a metallic wall. Only rich people could afford horses, so the cavalry was recruited from the corresponding strata. They carried two spears and a sword. Poor soldiers had no equipment. They fought as archers and carried slingshots with them.

The Athenians also had a stately navy. The ships were called **trireme**. They were equipped with three rows of straps and were rowed. At the bow there was a spur with which they rammed the enemy ships. Speed was the key to success. For this reason the Trireme had been developed from the original **diere** with two rows of straps.

14. The Medicine

The roots of modern medicine lie in ancient Greece. There was a traditional attitude that a god was responsible for the healing of a human being, namely **Asclepius**. The sick offered sacrifices to him and stayed overnight in the temple dedicated to him. They believed that he would visit them in a dream to heal them immediately or to show them the way to healing.

At the same time, however, a different direction was developing among the Greek doctors. They were looking for rational explanations for diseases and were using medical means to cure people.

Both ways of dealing with disease existed side by side, but the scientific direction was continuing to progress. Throughout Greece, including the colonies, schools of medicine were established to deal with the physical foundations of health and disease and to draw on appropriate ways of thinking. In 500 B.C., for example, there was the natural philosopher **Alcmaeon of Croton**, who regarded humans holistically. His thesis was that the body needs a healthy balance of heat and cold as well as dryness and wetness. As soon as the balance shifts, it reacts with discomfort and illness.

The most famous Greek doctor is **Hippocrates** (approx. 460–377 B.C.). He demanded that his professional colleagues observe the symptoms of the sick closely and draw conclusions from them. He refrained from invoking divine help in the treatment and relied on the healing power of plants. He was regarded as the founding father of modern medicine. The **Hippocratic Oath**, which became the moral basis of the medical profession, also originated with him.

There were also a number of Greek thinkers who started from an elementary structure of the body. If the elements were well balanced, they would assume that a person was healthy, but if they interfered in each of them, the person would become ill.

Aristotle (384–322 B.C.) gave medical thinking a further boost. He combined the secular elements water, fire, air and earth with the basic properties cold, warm, dry and humid and assumed that changes could occur within the elements. He transferred these qualities to the people to whom basic bodily fluids were assigned. He also assumed a fifth element which, unlike the others, was unchangeable, namely the ether.

The mindset of the four flexible elements eventually led to the **science of temperaments** established in antiquity. The human body and mind were seen in connection with each other. There were four types that have survived to this day as descriptions of characters:

Type	Saguinic	Choleric	Phlegmatic	Melancholic
Element	Air	Fire	Water	Earth
Property of the Element	Warm & Humid	Warm & Dry	Cold & Humid	Cold & Dry

Organ	Heart	Liver	Brain	Spleen
Body fluid	Blood	Yellow Bile	Phlegm	Black Bile
Characteristic of the body fluid	Light-blooded	Hot-blooded	Cumber-some	Melancholic
Personality	Spontaneous, Optimistic	Fast, Excitable and Quickly angry	Leisurely, Difficult to excite	Introverted, Pessimistic

The Greek doctors drew consequences from the types during the treatment. For example, if someone had a fever, he would have too much blood. The treatment would be bloodletting. The Greeks were also aware of the influence of diet, exercise and hygiene on health, and doctors began to pay attention to this in their patients.

15. Athens and Sparta

The two important city states developed very differently following the common victory over the Persians. The **Spartans** had **two kings** at their head. Even though from the 7th and 8th centuries B.C. the Council and the National Assembly were able to establish themselves as political authorities, the essential power lay in the hands of the regents, who, together with a select stratum, held power. Anyone who wanted to be politically active had to be a fully-fledged citizen and also possess real estate. This applied to free men in adulthood. They were called "**Spartiats**". Women, the perioeci people resident in the surrounding area (immigrant foreigners), and slaves were not among them. Despite the fact that women were politically treated as minors, they were emancipated in certain areas. Thus they were entitled to inherit their estates so that they did not have to fear for their livelihood after the loss of the male head of the family. They were also allowed to manage the house and farm because the men took care of the army's affairs or were at war.

In **Athens**, on the other hand, **Athenian democracy** unfolded, a further development of the democratic achievements of Cleisthenes. Areios Pagos or kings as rulers had long been a thing of the past. The constitution provided that the most important political organ was the **National Assembly**, where laws were decided and important officials elected or drawn by lot. The people were also responsible for whether there was war or peace. The organization of the administration was well thought out and effective in its implementation. The **Council** organized and chaired the National Assembly; it conducted the elections and votes. It was also the controlling authority for financial affairs and the administrative apparatus. It was guaranteed that citizens from all districts were represented in the Council. So that everyone could be politically active full-time, attendance was paid (with daily allowances or **regimens**). The **People's Court** had the judges drawn by lot. There were precautions that strengthened the legal system. Thus, the judges only became aware of the case at short notice in order to avoid any influence.

In the Athenian democracy, every adult citizen had the right to speak and the opportunity to be politically active. Women, metoecics and slaves were not considered citizens. Women in public office or as speakers were completely unthinkable. The higher ranked were allowed to educate themselves but only to have an opinion behind closed doors at home. Otherwise they were without rights.

The basic attitude towards life in Sparta was almost the opposite. In Sparta it was a matter of course to be raised militarily as a (male) child. A man was automatically a member of the army. To fall into the hands of enemy troops or to submit to them was a great disgrace. Then it was better to die for Sparta. Their whole life was therefore aligned to discipline, renunciation and heroism. Today we use the term "**Spartan people**" to refer to those who get along with little and accept hard living conditions.

The Athenians were very different. There was no professional army. The Athenians preferred to deal with the fine arts and detailed discussions about God and the world. They loved to philosophize and did so in public. They were interested in anything and everything. They made their lives as pleasant as possible. Those who could afford it decorated their houses with plenty of decorations.

The Spartans were at home in the **Peloponnese**, the peninsula of southern Greece. They were the inhabitants of the most spacious city state. They were able to do it without a protective masonry bulwark and their highly developed military was legendary. They were members of the **Pelopponesian League**, in which several cities of the region had joined together. The Spartans had a good reputation for their sense of proportion in their dealings with foreign countries. They knew little fear, but they were always concerned that the Athenians might be superior to them.

The Athenians had a city well protected by walls and a large area of the surrounding countryside as well as good access to the port, which they secured with a structure called the "**Long Walls**". They had the most inhabitants. Their union was the **Delian League**, a union with the coastal towns. It helped to ensure that Athens had a stable position and was able to increase its prosperity.

16. The Pelopponesian War

Between Athens and Sparta there were always disputes. In 461 B.C., the Athenians provoked Sparta by breaking the Hellenic League and allying themselves with the cities of Megara and Argos. They had also succeeded in conquering some cities on the coasts, giving them great power. Sparta then allied itself with Thebes. In the period **from 457 to 445 B.C.** there were warlike conflicts between Athens and Sparta. This phase is called the **First Pelopponesian War**. At the end there was a peace treaty. The statesman **Pericles** from Athens negotiated it with the Spartans. It included the agreement on 30 years of peace between Sparta and Athens and the assurance of mutual respect for the respective allies. Megara was returned again to Sparta. The city states, which were independent and not affiliated to either of the two great powers, remained unaffected by the treaty. In fact, in the following years there were frictions but no acts of war.

But it came to the **Second Pelopponesian War from 431 to 404 B.C.** Corinth was an ally of Sparta. This city was striving for more power, especially in the Ionian Sea, and was arming its warships enormously. The Athenians saw this as a threat to their own powerful position and, as a precaution, formed an alliance with the enemy of the Corinthians, Kerkyra (today's Corfu). However, Corinth interpreted this as a breach of the peace treaty and ordered Sparta to keep Athens in check. A conflict between Sparta and Athens arose, during which Athens imposed a trade embargo on Megara, a member of the Pelopponesian League. King **Archidamos II of Sparta** did not want to be a warmonger, but he could not escape the pressure. The Spartans saw themselves threatened by the Athenians. It came to a war.

Phase 1: Archidamian War (431–421 B.C.)

The Spartans mobilized their forces under the guise of fighting for freedom and autonomy, but their real motivation was their desire for power. They had a strong army superior to the Athenians with their phalanx tactics on the mainland. Therefore, they strived to defeat the enemy by land. But the Athenians had built the Long Walls behind which they were retreating. The Spartans repeated the attack for several years, destroying a lot of agricultural land. Only the two years in which an epidemic spread and an earthquake raged were left out. The Athenians wanted to avoid a battle on land and achieve victory with their superior fleet. They attacked the coastal towns that belonged to Sparta and caused the Spartans a seaway blockade. Both powers relied on an attrition tactic that was supposed to annoy the other, and both failed because of this.

In the year 429, the leading statesman Pericles died and in Athens two political directions developed. **Cleon** was one of the radical representatives who wanted to destroy Sparta, while **Nicias** advised a diplomatic solution with

Sparta. Sparta renounced further invasions of the Athenian countryside because this tactic had led to too many losses. The Athenians were attacked on the outskirts. General **Brasidas** had allied with the king of Macedonia and could therefore cause serious damage to Athens. He won victories in areas that guaranteed the Athenians had access to their grain resources. However, Cleon continued to fight Sparta and was killed in the **Battle of Amphipolis** in **422 B.C.** Brasidas scored an outstanding victory but also lost his life. After the death of the two hardliners, the end of the war could be envisaged.

Phase 2: Nicias' peace (421–413 B.C.)

In the year 421 B.C., the peace treaty was concluded, which was to be valid for 50 years. It stated that Athens would release the captured warriors from Sparta and leave some strategically advantageous places on the Peloppones, while Sparta would march out of comparable areas in Thrace. But neither Athens nor Sparta kept to the agreements. They did not give up important military stations, which led to disagreements on both sides. At the same time, the Corinthians and Thebanians were indignant because they were ignored in the agreement. There were conflicts in the Pelopponesian Confederation. An alliance was formed against the parties, including the cities of Corinth and Argos, but it could not last because Athens and Sparta were once again politically active. The Athenian statesman **Alcibiades** succeeded in pulling Argos to his side, while Sparta again joined forces with Thebes and Corinth.

Alcibiades didn't think much of Nicias' peace-building political style and wanted to help Athens gain more power and prosperity. To this end he planned to conquer Sicily, a stately Greek granary. In order to enforce this against Nicias, he used his popularity at the National Assembly, which he inspired for the action. In 415 B.C., Alcibiades and Nicias moved an enormous number of troops towards Syracuse on the coast of Sicily. But Alcibiades achieved a recall to Athens. He was to answer to the court for religious misconduct. He was accused of demolishing Hermes figures and blasphemy. To escape the prosecution, he took the side of Sparta who helped Syracuse. The Athenians were defeated in the **battle for Syracuse**. The soldiers died or were captured; Nicias was executed. This devastating campaign proved fateful for Athens. It never returned to its old strength.

Phase 3: The Decelean War (413–404 B.C)

Athens and Sparta continued to be enemies. Athens was attacked in some areas, which Sparta interpreted as a breach of the Nicias Peace Treaty and in turn returned to attack. Alcibiades selected the strategically advantageous town of Decelea, where Sparta built a military base and overlooked the Athenian territory. From there it controlled Athens, which was cut off from its supply lines. There was only the road across the sea and the island of Euboea to secure agricultural products and food supplies. The Athenians had also driven the Persians into the arms of Sparta by supporting insurgents against the Persian Empire. The Persians and Spartans made mutual gains, while the Delian League—due to the weakness of Athens—suffered from membership loss. Sparta left Asia Minor to the Persians and received in return financial means with which it made its warships float again.

The difficult situation of the Athenians led to thoughts of revolution in the course of the unfavorable development. Some oligarchs overruled the constitution and the National Assembly. Again Alcibiades played an important role. Meanwhile, unpopular with the Spartans, he served the oligarchic agitators by convincing them that they would come to terms with the Persians again as the new rulers of Athens. He wanted to return to Athens himself. They went into it but unsuccessfully. Peace came neither with Sparta nor with the Persians, and the constitution, including the National Assembly, came into force again. Alcibiades had changed sides again in time and had become the leader of the democratic movement. As commander-in-chief he won several victories over the Spartans and became commander-in-chief of the entire army. But in the **Battle of Notium 407 B.C.** the Spartans won, thanks to their competent General **Lysander** and the help from Persia. Alcibiades was put on the political sidelines.

In **406 B.C.**, the **Arginusae** Islands near Lesbos were the scene of a gigantic naval battle between Sparta and Athens, the likes of which had never been seen before. The Athenians won the battle but brought their own important commanders to justice, who had been unable to save many shipwrecked soldiers due to a storm. They were sentenced to death, which considerably weakened the competence of the fleet. Athens defeated the Spartans led by Lysander at the **Battle of Aegospotami in 405 B.C.** but had to capitulate a year later. Athens escaped destruction, but the Long Walls were torn down. The League of the Sea was abolished and only came into being decades later, far less influentially. The Golden Age ended for the Athenians in 404 B.C.

17. Transition to the Rise of Macedonia

But the Spartans were not satisfied. Over the next few years they threw themselves over with their allies because they wanted to expand their dominions. Around the year 400, the conflict with the Persians began again. Sparta lost influence between the various political alliances and claims to power. In addition, it was not defeated in the **Corinthian War (395–387 B.C.)** with Argos, Athens, Thebes and Corinth, but its resources were weakened. At the end of the war there was **royal peace**, which granted Asia Minor and Cyprus to the Persians and granted independence to the Greek mainland city states. But since the Spartans were to control the guarantee of the agreements, they used this to strengthen their political position again. In return, Athens constituted the second Athenian League and approached the influential Thebes. Thebes defeated the Spartans in the **Battle of Leuctra in 371 B.C.**, thus severely weakening Sparta. The political situation with alliances and counter-alliances became completely unclear for several years. In the end, after the **Battle of Mantinea in 362 B.C.**, led against Sparta and its allies and in which it lost its grandiose commander, Thebes also had to give up its supremacy.

In the following years there were further violent arguments between Sparta and Thebes, whereby both powers suffered disadvantages.

Athens experienced a new economic and cultural upswing and felt so strengthened that it formed an alliance against the powerful Macedonia, known as the **Chalkidic League**. He declared war on **Philip II of Macedonia** but was defeated in the **Battle of Chaeronea** in 338 B.C. One year later, the Macedonian ruler founded the **Corinthian League**, in which all Greek city states united under his leadership. He was then the master of the most powerful empire in Europe. His declared aim was to subjugate the Persians. But before he could become active, he was murdered in the year **336 B.C**. His son, **Alexander the Great**, inherited the kingdom.

18. Alexander the Great (356–323 B.C.)

a) The First Years

Alexander the Great became king immediately after the death of his father. He later received the epithet of the Great for his brilliant military abilities but also for the great diplomatic skill he showed in dealing with the conquered countries and their people. After all, he marched into almost all areas of the known world at that time. Thus he spread the Greek culture, language and world view in Asia Minor, Egypt and Mesopotamia over Central Asia to India. He always had scientists with him who carried out botanical, zoological, meteorological and geological studies of the new regions. This was where the influence of his great mentor **Aristotle**, whom Philip II had engaged for the education and upbringing of young people, made him noticed.

In addition to reading and writing, Alexander also learned to play the lyre. His penchant for music and literature remained with him throughout his life. He was often seen with books under his arm. Of course he also learned to fight and to harden himself. Long marches formed part of his education. He was an exceptional intellectual with a high level of education, robust health and a large portion of willpower. His military skills and bravery appeared early. In the Battle of Chaeronea he had fought as an eighteen-year-old and contributed to the victory.

Alexander saw his success not as a result of his education but as divine destiny. He claimed himself to be a **son of the father of the god Zeus** and thus rose to the appearance of a demigod—an attitude which his mother had encouraged from an early age. At the age of 12 he was said to have succeeded in taming a horse considered to be untameable, but this has not been clearly proven. The "**Gordian Knot**" was also a legend. In the city of Gordion, Alexander was said to have cut a very complex knot in a car with a sword because an oracle had prophesied that the one who could undo the knot would become ruler over Asia.

b) The Battle of Issus

In **334 B.C.**, Alexander moved to Asia Minor and liberated the Greek city of Ephesus from Persian rule. In 333 B.C., he defeated the troops of the **Persian leader Darius III in the Battle of Issus**. Darius escaped and Alexander was able to seize the cities of Sidon (today's Lebanon) and Aleppo (today's Syria) and thus ruled the coast of Phoenicia (eastern Mediterranean coast). He rejected Darius III's proposal to divide the territory. One year later, he brought Syria under control and conquered Egypt, where he founded **Alexandria** and was proclaimed pharaoh. Here he proved his enormous ability to control large areas. He refrained from imposing Greek culture on the Egyptians as long as they were prepared to keep the supply lines open for his army to make supplies possible and to provide food for people and animals. This was an aspect that the subsequent warlords neglected. Insurgents and all who opposed his plans fought Alexander ruthlessly. He wanted to conquer the Phoenician trading town of **Tyros**, which at that time was situated on a small island, and initially offered protection on surrender. But the Tyrians resisted. Alexander had dams built to reach them, conquered them and forced the survivors into slavery.

c) The Persian War

In 331 B.C., Alexander set out again against the Persian king Darius III, who in the meantime had built up a new army of far more than 200,000 men and also moved in with elephants. Alexander's army consisted of slightly more than 40,000 men, including the mounted soldiers. Through his war tactics to attack directly the center of the opponent, he won the important **Battle of Gaugamela**. Darius escaped for the second time but was later murdered. Alexander punished the murderer, had Darius honorably buried and tried to establish a close connection with the Persian nobility, which he needed as allies for his rule over the Persians. This earned him the wrath of some officers, whom he mercilessly punished. He appointed himself as the **king of Asia** and moved against **Susa** (city in today's Iran), who submitted without a fight. From there he continued to **Persepolis**, which he largely destroyed. In 329 B.C., he founded the city of Alexandria-Eschate and subdued Sogdia (Central Asia). He named other cities after him, e.g. Alexandria at the Hindu Kush. With this he wanted to promote his reputation as a deity. He introduced his soldiers to the Persian custom of falling to their knees in front of him and kissing his hand before they spoke to him. His behavior led to conspiracies against him, which, however, were discovered and severely punished. Although Alexander was known for being diplomatic with the inhabitants of the conquered territories, he did not tolerate anyone who contradicted his views. The same applied to his friends. When General **Cleitus** accused him of cowardice in an argument, he murdered him, although he had been his companion for many years and had even saved his life in a battle. He regretted this later, especially since he had been drunk during the fight. Alexander was known for alcohol excesses.

d) The India Campaign

In 327 B.C., Alexander completely controlled the Persian Empire. His attention was focused on India, of which little was known at the time. **Omphis**, the king of **Taxila** (now eastern Afghanistan and northwestern Pakistan), had heard of his deeds and submitted without a fight. Alexander conquered the area from Kabul to the Indus in 326 B.C. and appointed a governor there. In the India campaign, in which no other motive could be recognized than an urge to conquer, Alexander became more and more unyielding against his subjects and left his tolerant nature untouched. He challenged the countries of the **Punjab** (located in today's Pakistan and India) to submit to him as a deity. King **Poros** refused and was fought. In the **Battle of Hydaspes** Alexander defeated the Indians but had to accept high losses as well. He made Poros his governor in his previous kingdom.

Alexander wanted to move on and cross the **Ganges** to conquer more areas, but his army refused to follow him in the face of the agonizing monsoon and numerous losses. He was forced to return home. Before that he founded another Alexandria, in which he left a part of his soldiers for settlement. On his way home he fought several more battles, partly because he was threatened and partly because he himself attacked again. He had unfaithful governors executed, whom he had used on his campaign and who he found to be abusing his power. During his journey home, he attempted to unite his soldiers with the inhabitants of Persia so that the cultures of Macedonia and Persia would mix with each other and the peoples would come together. He even arranged a **massive wedding** in Susa, where he married his veterans to noble women. He married two high-ranking Persians and, now with three wives, followed the example of his father, who used polygamy as a means of political consolidation. However, his troops did not live up to his ambitions and rejected Persian culture. He presented himself more as a Persian king and less as a Macedonian king.

e) After Returning Home

When Alexander's long-time friend and combat companion **Hephaestion** died of a fever in the winter of 323 B.C., he fell into a severe crisis. He had the attending doctor crucified. It took a long time before he became active again. Economically he promoted trade on land and at sea by converting the treasures of the Persian royalty into funds. In this way the Mediterranean trade grew enormously. In the year **324 B.C.** he initiated an innovation for the Olympic Games. The city states of Greece had to reinstate their political emigrants who had been sent into exile. This was a big break in the self-administration and proved to be one of the reasons why many cities rebelled against the power of Macedonia in the **Lamian War** (323–322 B.C.), although they remained unsuccessful. Alexander died before the uprising of a fever, the cause of which remains historically unclear.

XV. The Hellenistic Period (336–30 B.C.)

1. The Diadochian Wars

The death of Alexander the Great left a great gap in the leadership of the vast empire. His closest relative, **Perdiccas**, wanted to take the lead and hold it together, but the other Diadochi (Alexander the Great's commanders and their sons) turned against him. There were several **Diadochian wars**, which ended in 311 B.C. in the **Diadochian peace**. There were then three large Hellenistic empires that could stabilize Greece.

The **Ptolemies Empire** included Egypt, Cyprus, parts of Asia Minor and the Mediterranean coast as well as Cyrene (in today's Libya). The capital, the Egyptian Alexandria, had sovereignty over the approximately 40 provinces, each of which was administered by a tax official. There was an effective procedure for levying taxes.

The **Seleucid Empire** covered large parts of Asia. It was ruled by a king and was based on the social structure of the Persians. The territory of the empire was divided into districts headed by an administrator. The king had a "Vizier" as the highest administrator to the side. The inhabitants of the empire consisted of very different strata of the population with different cultural backgrounds, all of which, however, knew only one monarchical rule as a political regime. Therefore, they could be held together relatively easily.

The **Antigonid Empire** consisted of Macedonia and large parts of Greece. They held on to polis.

2. The Fall of Ancient Greece

The Antigonid Empire consisted of Macedonia and large parts of Greece. They held on to polis. The Hellenistic empires were not satisfied with their state of affairs, but all sought to expand their dominions. Thus the **six Syrian wars** between the Egyptian Ptolemies and the Seleucids took place between **274 and 168 B.C.**, each with interruptions. The main focus was on the important eastern Mediterranean coast with its hinterland. From the fifth war onwards the Ptolemies were confronted not only with the Seleucids but also with the strong **Roman Republic** and **Macedonia under the rule of Philip V**. They had to hand over their Asian territories to the Seleucid king **Antiochus III** and the Egyptian Ptolemies became dependent on Rome. In the sixth war the Ptolemaic Egyptians again fought against the Seleucids, but at the same time a **battle took place between the Roman Republic and Macedonia**. The result was that Macedonia and Greece became provinces of the overpowering Rome. Although the Seleucids defeated the

Ptolemies, this did not help them because the Romans treated Egypt as a protectorate.

All Hellenistic empires were hardly able to wage war on their own. Rome conquered power in the eastern Mediterranean and continued to advance. Corinth was defeated, and in **146 B.C.** the Romans made Greece their province. **Thus ancient Greece became history**. In **30 B.C.** Rome annexed the Ptolemaic Empire as the last Hellenistic territory, and the Hellenistic period suffered the same fate. But the high culture of the ancient Greeks could be found in many areas of the Romans so that it was by no means lost. However, an autonomous state of Greece was not to exist until centuries later.

XVI. The Mythology of the Ancient Greeks

From mythology the Greeks learned that the gods determined the course of the world. They had a decisive influence on the fate of mankind and sometimes even intervened directly. Human beings had to make sacrifices for them so that they remained well-disposed towards them. Essentially, it was not the will of the people that determined what happened but the guidance of the gods. Those who were particularly gifted, for example as doctors or lecturers, had received their gift from the gods.

The great heroes of Greek mythology, such as **Hercules**, who was endowed with giant powers, the invincible **Achilles** or **Jason**, who led the Argonauts in search of the Golden Fleece, were the descendants of gods. Thus mythology connected the gods with the human world and gave people examples of exemplary behavior. Hercules had to accomplish 12 difficult tasks, including killing a monster with newly growing heads, the "**Hydra**". People were expected to strive for such ideals. But it was also shown that misconduct did not go unpunished, e.g. passing fire on to humans, for which the god Prometheus was banished to a rock by Zeus, the father of the gods. **King Midas**' greed was punished by fulfilling his wish that everything he touched would turn into gold. Midas had to starve because he could not eat or drink gold. Narcissus lost his will to live because of his vanity, which led him to fall in love with his own reflection.

Natural phenomena were mythologically explained. Earthquakes occurred when **Poseidon** rammed his trident into the seabed, and the sun's migration occurred because **Helios** was driving his car along the sky. But mythology also included strange creatures. There was the one-eyed Cyclops, which Odysseus defeated with cunning, huge snakes, sphinxes, fire breathing bulls and the **centaur**, who is half human and half horse. **Perseus** had to behead the "**Medusa**", whose glances petrified a man.

One of the great myths was the **Trojan War**. The ancient Greeks assumed that it had taken place in the 13th century B.C. In their imagination, **Zeus** wanted to bring back his daughter **Helena**, whom the Trojan Prince **Paris** had taken with him. She had been promised to him by **Aphrodite**, whom he had chosen as the winner of a beauty contest among three female deities. Thus began the war of the Greeks against the Trojans, led by the royal hero **Odysseus** of Ithaca. Especially spectacular was his trick with which he invaded the Trojan city. While the victory was already being celebrated, the Greeks set up a wooden horse—**the "Trojan Horse"**—in front of the city walls, in which their soldiers were hiding. As expected, the Trojans grabbed the entity and sealed their fate. The soldiers opened the gates and the drunken Trojans were quickly overwhelmed. Helena was brought back. But the journey home turned out to be a bad one. Odysseus needed ten years to complete it because the gods also wanted to punish him because of some iniquities and sent thunderstorms and other obstacles. Back home, he killed the men who wanted to marry his wife **Penelope** and took over the rule himself. Motifs from the Trojan War can be found in pottery, sculpture and painting.

XVII. The Oracle of Delphi

The Oracle of Delphi spoke for the god **Apollo**. It mainly answered questions about colonization, religion and power. His prophecies made Delphi a rich and important city. The oracle was in its golden period in 1600 B.C. and was forbidden in 391 A.D., like other oracles, by **Emperor Theodosius I**, who was a Christian ruler.

The oracle was called **Pythia** and was always a woman because it was originally assigned to the goddess Gaia. Basically every woman was allowed to become an oracle; it depended solely on her gift to speak for the god. However, a married woman could not perform her duties well because she would be neglecting her domestic duties. The Pythia had to undergo a ritual washing before being questioned. With a laurel crown on her head, she sat on a three-legged stool in front of the Apollo altar in the temple of the god. According to tradition, a vault underneath the temple was filled with steam, which put her into a trance. To this day it is unclear whether they contained mind-altering substances and whether she gave her answers by hallucination or whether the priests present whispered the words to her. What is certain is that she spoke a few sentences for the richer, well-paying people, but these were usually very difficult to interpret, while poor questioners only received a yes or no. According to a prominent myth, she predicted that **Oedipus** would murder his father and marry his mother. In order to avoid this, Oedipus suffered exactly this fate. Hence the term **"Oedipus complex"** coined by the psychologist Sigmund Freud.

XVIII. Famous Greeks

1. The Archaic Period

At the beginning of Greek history, the Archaic Period produced a grandiose literary achievement, the epics *Iliad* **and** *Odyssey of Homer*. Little is known about the poet, not even his place of birth is clear. There are different opinions as to whether he wrote these cultural-historical documents alone or whether he did so with help. Whether the Trojan War, the theme of the narratives, actually took place, has also been disputed. However, both works were recognized as historical sources to the extent that much of the life of that time could be reconstructed from them.

Besides Homer, **Hesiod (approx. 700 B.C.)** was the most famous poet of early Greece. He wrote instructions in poem form, which was called the form of "teaching poem". His great works were *Theogony* and *Works and Days*. From them was taken essential knowledge about the mythology of the Greeks. Also the **"Pandora's Box"**, which is still used today as a saying for a bad fate, comes from his story. At that time he propagated a **work ethic** by emphasizing how important it is to create something with one's own hands. In doing so, he indirectly distanced himself from the aristocracy, which acquired its possessions through inheritance.

Pythagoras (approx. 571—497 B.C.) was a philosopher. He came from the island of Samos. Much of what concerns his teachings remains approximate because reliable sources are lacking. It is agreed that he belonged to the great thinkers. It is uncertain whether his insights beyond mathematics also relate to philosophy and the natural sciences. In any case, he founded a union in which his followers, the Pythagoreans, met. They imposed a system of rules on themselves as to how they should behave in everyday life and celebrated religious acts about which they kept strict silence. It has been proven that they were not only religious but also politically engaged. We still apply the "**Pythagorean theorem**" today.

Thales of Miletus (approx. 624–548 B.C.) was regarded as the first Western philosopher and scholar of astronomy, mathematics and geometry, and he was also politically active. His theories were not preserved in written form, but much of his great knowledge was recorded and passed on by contemporaries. It is assumed that he had exact astronomical knowledge and predicted the **solar eclipse of 585 B.C.** exactly. After Aristotle he was the first to ask about the origin of being. He came to the conclusion that it must be water because it is the only element that can change its shape without changing its substance.

2. The Classical Period

Herodotus (approx. 484–approx. 425) was a far-reaching historian. With his explanations about historical events he founded the science that has been called "history" since then. The famous Roman lecturer Cicero called him "father of history". In his great work ***Histories*** he described the Persian Empire. We also thank him for his knowledge of the Persian wars and the details of the Battle of Salamis.

Democritus (approx. 460–370 B.C.) was a Greek philosopher and scholar. Together with his mentor Leucippus he assumed that the natural world consisted of tiny indivisible parts, the atoms. He also developed mathematical, physical, medical, ethical and astrological theories. Among the latter was his postulate that the Milky Way consists of the light of stars that reach our senses and that we live in a multiverse in which there are also planets with other life forms—a theory that scientists of our time deal with! Democritus was given the nickname **"the smiling philosopher"** because he regarded serenity as the ideal attitude to life.

Aristophanes (approx. 450–380 B.C.) was the famous comedy poet of antiquity. His innovative and sometimes quite popular portrayals often contained satirical content with taunts against the ruling elite. For example, he thematized cultural changes and the role of women. Many references to the legal and religious practices of the time could be found in his work. The expressions "**Cloud cuckoo land**" and "**Taking owls to Athens**" (or "carrying coals to Newcastle") originated from his writing.

The three most famous playwrights of the Greek Classical Period:

- Some dramas by **Aeschylus (525–456 B.C.)** have survived, including the *Oresteia*, which is still performed today.

- **Sophocles (approx. 497–406 B.C.)** was one of the most famous poets of antiquity. His tragedies were world literature, including *King Oedipus*, and his dramas, including *Electra*. Many of his works are still performed worldwide today. They bear witness to the theatrical events of antiquity, but they also provide a great deal of insight into the lives of people at that time. The political and social conditions are expressed as well as the family structures and details of religious customs.

- **Euripides (480 to 484 B.C.)** wrote dozens of tragedies, 18 of which have survived. He is still one of the great poets brought to the stage today, including *Medea* and also a play called *Electra*.

The three most famous philosophers of the Greek Classical Period:

- **Socrates (469–399 B.C.)** philosophized in detail about how one can lead a good and virtuous life. Unfortunately, no documents have survived. According to Plato, he was very disappointed that many respected men, who were said to have wisdom, did not have it, while others, who were looked down upon, were much more reasonable. He came to this view after having many conversations. The reason was that his friend had asked the Oracle of Delphi if there was anyone wiser than Socrates. Pythia had denied it, and he wanted to refute this. Socrates made many speeches in which he asked people to think for themselves and not always follow the given social conventions. He also called for resistance against superstition.

The youth listened to him carefully when he proclaimed his wisdom in the Athens marketplace. He loved to conduct dialogues and established a method for doing so. He said, "**I know I don't know anything,**" because despite all the studies you can't be sure you have the right knowledge. He was sentenced to death because he incited youth and denied the gods. Still in captivity and until the last minute, before he drank the deadly cup of hemlock, he was holding discussions with his followers. Since Socrates is considered a great philosopher whose ideas influenced the following centuries, philosophy before him is called **pre-Socratic**.

- **Plato (428–348 B.C.)** was a student of Socrates. He was very impressed by the life of his teacher and his death burdened him heavily. He recorded the defence speech before the People's Court under the title "**The Apology of Socrates**". In his writings he made use of dialogue. There were theses and counter theses, questions and counter questions and open problems in the constant struggle for the truth. Plato argued that truth lies in the realm of original images and forms, of which the human senses perceive only a kind of reflection. If, for example, someone looks at a horse and finds it "beautiful", he or she is talking about how strongly the horse is connected to the original idea of beauty.

The part of the human being that has access to this world of ideas is the **soul**. It alone can at least partially claim the knowledge of what really exists. For human action, Plato was concerned with the realization of how difficult it is to distinguish a pure opinion from generally established knowledge. On the one hand, man should recognize that he hardly really knows anything, and on the other hand he should always strive for truth and higher things. He should not simply believe anything unchecked. Plato was the first to create a school of philosophy, the **"Platonic Academy" in Athens**. It became the starting point for the spread of his theories, which in the following centuries became part of Western philosophy. Plato was an allround talent and also studied art, language, anthropology and cosmology. Several of his works have survived, including the philosophical conversation "**Phaedo**" and the political writings "**The Laws**" and "**The State**".

- **Aristotle (384–322 B.C.)** was a student of Plato. He was regarded as a pioneer in the systematic, exact investigation of the connections between many sciences, from biology, physics, mathematics and logic to politics, philosophy, literature and theater studies. He also created important foundations for the field of rhetoric, which found widespread use in the ancient world through him. In his time he was called the **"man who knows everything"**. He studied at Plato's Academy and remained there for 20 years as a teacher. Then he became a mentor for **Alexander the Great**. He introduced him to art and cultural techniques and taught him diplomatic and rhetorical skills. He remained connected with his famous student through letters even after Alexander had long since become a conqueror of other countries.

Aristotle returned to Athens after Alexander's education and became Plato's rival. He created his own school, the **Lyceum ("Lykeion")**. While Plato argued that the truth could not be extracted from experiments, Aristotle said the opposite. He assumed that the visible and observable things could be explored and that the research led to an underlying, recognizable cause. He expressly did not share the idea that truth lies in a higher, invisible plan that is only partially accessible to the soul. Aristotle owed much of his knowledge to formal logic, rhetoric, the natural sciences, political science and philosophy. The basic observation that matter can take on different forms can be traced back, for example, to him. For the coexistence of human beings, he postulated a **theory of forms of government** that for centuries was regarded as irrefutable. He started from the necessity of a political constitution in order to make a happy life possible for the individual. Teachers and educators, he believed, should shape the character of a child by strengthening virtuous action, reason and understanding, and control over feelings.

3. The Hellenistic Period

Euclid of Alexandria (approx. 300 B.C.) was the first to compile and systematize the mathematical knowledge of his time. He did the same with geometry. He wrote the book **Elements** in which he presented the collected knowledge. There were already fundamental thoughts about **prime numbers** and the necessity of logical proof in mathematics. The western science of mathematics refers to Euclid in the following centuries until the modern age, where his theses were often confirmed and further developed, others were also refuted.

Archimedes (approx. 287–212 B.C.) was one of the most important mathematicians and physicists of antiquity, to whom many scientific findings can be traced back. He also worked as an engineer, designing war weapons among other things. These included catapults used in the **Punic Wars** (a series of wars between 264 and 146 B.C. between Carthage and the strengthening and ultimately victorious Roman Empire). Legend had it that one day he walked through the streets completely undressed and

said, "Eureka!" (English:"I found it") because he had made a profound discovery. This exclamation has survived to this day.

Legal notice and disclaimer

This work including all its contents is protected by copyright. Reproduction, in whole or in part, as well as storage, processing, duplication and distribution by means of electronic systems, in whole or in part, is forbidden without the written permission of the Author. All translation Rights reserved.

The contents of this book were searched on the basis of recognized sources and examined with utmost care. However, the Author assumes no guarantee regarding the timeliness, accuracy and completeness of the information provided.

Liability claims against the author relating to the damages of any health, material or ideal nature caused by the use or non-use of the information provided for or by the use of incorrect and incomplete information are in principle excluded, so far, removed from the Author. Intentionally or grossly negligent. This book does not replace medical or professional advice and care.

www.ingramcontent.com/pod-product-compliance
Lightning Source LLC
LaVergne TN
LVHW010649200726
843507LV00011B/1787